Today's
Reflections

Today's *Reflections*

Ellie's Little Scribbles

Charles W. Hull

EDITED BY
Paula Stahel

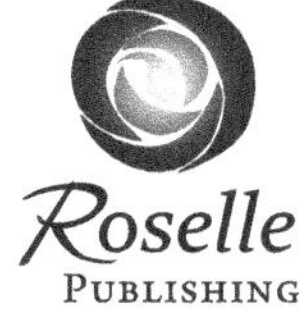

Roselle
PUBLISHING

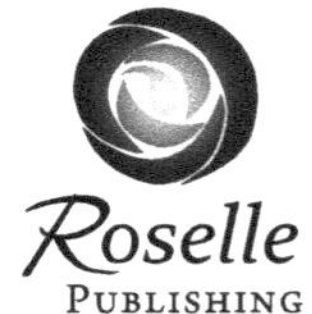

Roselle
PUBLISHING

Today's Reflections – Ellie's Little Scribbles by Charles W. Hull

Book Design: Denise Borel Billups, Borel Graphics
Editor: Paula Stahel, Breath & Shadows Productions

ISBN 978-0-9968109-0-6
Library of Congress
Cataloging-in-Publication Data
2018943668
Cover and interior photographs
courtesy of Charles W. Hull
Flying 101 photo courtesy of Catherine Frey

DEDICATED TO
McDONALD ALSTON HULL (HANNIBAL),
MY BROTHER AND POET.

"Today is not the day I
dreamed of yesterday
Today I'm so blue
Today is not the day I
dreamed of yesterday
'cause I'm not with you"

**From "At The Crossroads"
with permission of the heirs of
McDonald Alston Hull**

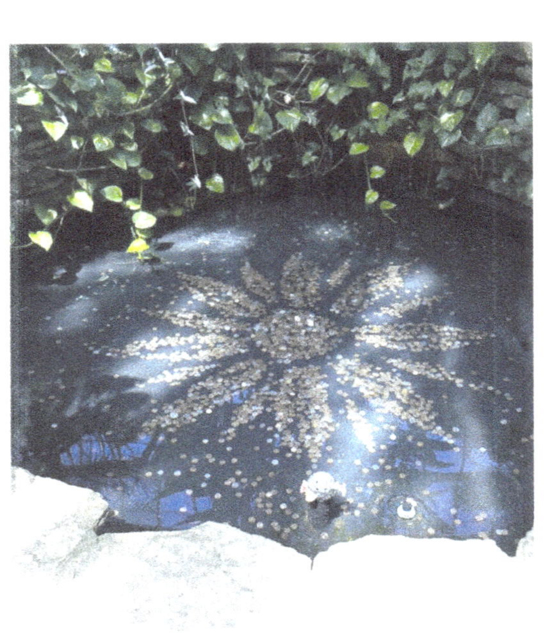

Contents

– Lagniappe –
(Freebie)
Poetry Through the Lens

FOREWORD

There are times in your life, when,
unbidden, random thoughts
pop into your mind
or float just below your consciousness.
You follow them where they may lead,
untrammeled by any direction
on your part.

It may be sitting in a supermarket
in Sweden, left to your own devices while
the ladies go shopping. It may be the
heart-rending grief expressed by one who
loses the husband and son,
both unexpectedly in sleep or by accident.
It may also be as simple a thing as fruit
hanging from the branch
of a potted plant.

All these set off threads, words and
feelings, which come forth and need to be
set down on pads, on scraps of paper;
these little scribbles which define us,

coming from deep within,
pushing their slender threads up
to the light.

Sometimes they come full circle and
you see the thought, the imaginings,
physically expressed as you walk
along a flower-strewn path.

Then you read your brother's poems and
realize that we all see the same things
but differently — yesterday, today,
everyday

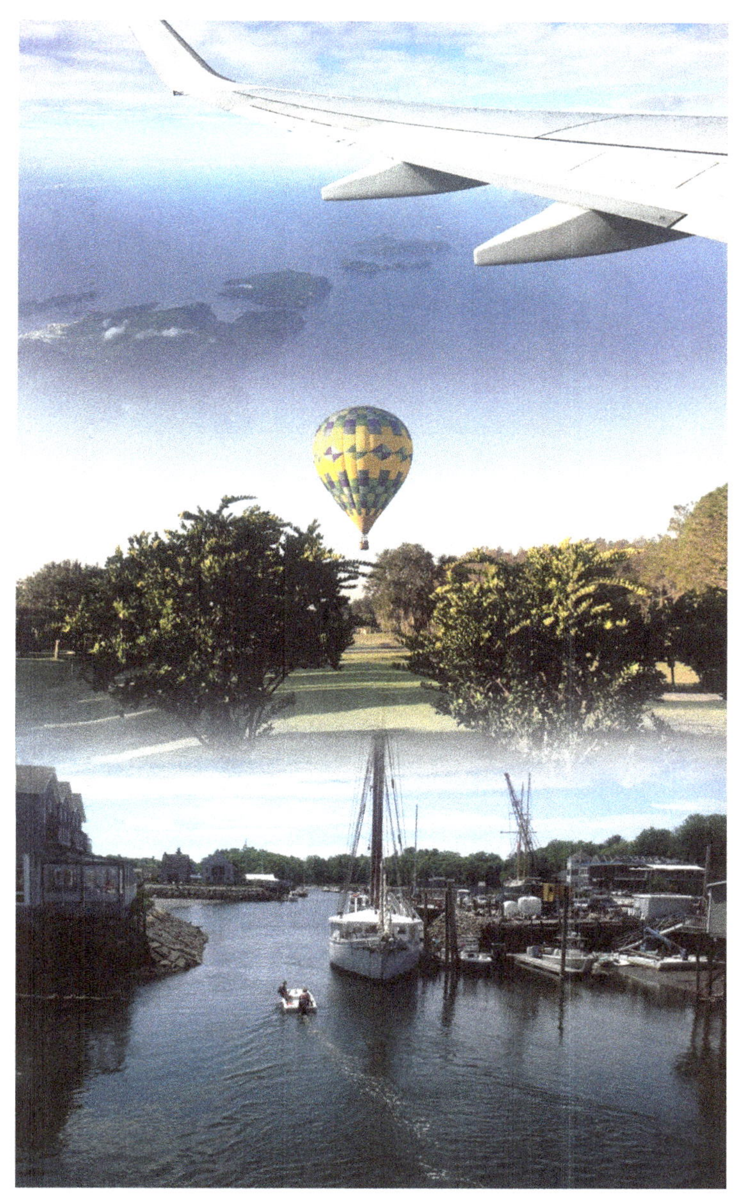

– DISCOVERY –

Faces, Faces, Different Faces

Is this Sweden?
We think of blonde and Nordic
We see dark hair and Slavic
"Hallal" the sign says
Muslim we think, Kosovo the link
The grace, the beauty, tall and slim
I pause, but no, the waddling,
thickening
Misconceptions, misperceptions,
Expectations
No golden gods and goddesses
No au pairs of London fame
Just folk, simple folk
They play, they work, they ride, they
bike
Leather jackets for tough bikers
Just jackets for us pikers

Today

Today I saw a deer
Tip-toeing across the green grass
To sip and sup without fear
From bowl on lawn so green
Today I saw a dog
A funny sight that, sitting on front seat
Driven by Mom, talking, talking,
chatting, chatting
Dog nodding, nodding, listening,
listening

Today I heard the news
Today I heard a plane, swooping,
soaring, droning high
Today I heard the news
Bombs away, Iraq no less, five
hundred gone, God Bless
Today I saw a truck all red
Today I heard one dead
Driving, crashing, highway bound;
he leaps, he darts, he cares
Honey are you OK? Oh no he's down,
eternally at rest
We feed the deer
Drive the dog
Kill her dear
Bomb the wog
Do we really care?

Explorer

A voyage of discovery said Columbus
Travel afar says regius
Go west to east with arquebus
Seek fame and fortune for us
Sailing, sailing, tossing, rolling
Becalmed at times, winds swirling
Land ho, land ho, he hails
Iere fair, beyond the waves
Zach we sought, down south
The curves, the turns, far from north
The hill we spy, our final port
Mango tree, poui, ancestral thought
A voyage of discovery, said Phil
Go forth afar, Caillie to seek
Of him they speak, words so sweet
Ancient lips, tales to speak
Ancient memories of travels afar
Visits to Dora with Granma
By train, by road, hand held tight
Lord, the tunnel, no light in sight
Images viewed by night
Photos taken at daylight
Dates recorded, ever lost
Timeless villages, fluttering moths
A voyage of discovery says Ellie
The land of milk and honey
Jostling, jostling, changing, changing

Narrow paths, cars preening, ever careening
Birds flying in and out
Screeching, chirping, twitting loud
We snooze, we wake, quick, quick
Rise aloft on wings, eyes to hills
Old friends to meet, drink and greet
New friends to make, on the beach
Towers high, new born arise
Home team, your leader dies
Fading photos, deeds of lands
Memories of carnival bands
Steel band symphony, classic tones
Radio waves, all moans
Brave Columbus sailed away
Another voyage, someday, one day
Ellie by night, no light, climbs aloft
and turns
Phil fulfilled, searching, seeking,
returns, returns

My Brother's Keeper

We sit here in the morning sunlight
Red streaked clouds in the sky
Droplets hanging, glinting off the tips
Of little leaves, succulents in the
gravel bed
It grows from tiny seed, clayey soil,
gravel overlain
Lay dormant for a long while,
we despair will it ever rise
But lo, years later it blooms,
flourishing water nurtured
Grows too much perhaps but beauty in
its quiet lowly self
Brilliant sunshine, bright stunning
orb pours through
Warming the brow, rays all round
blue heavenly vault
The bird croaks and squawks, no
twitter, just calling
Announcing the break of day,
thank God for life
Eye resting near, a man, a stick,
a bag, ancient bowl in hand
Sitting on his brother's shoulders,
travelling ancient roads

Perhaps tis his son bearing him,
travelling on a dusty way
From ancient Africa the message,
I am my brother's keeper
Twisted rope, hand carved dark
beauteous wood
Fruit in panniers borne on
asses' backs. Heads
Held high all tied, proudly walking
tugging child. Tree of life
Spreading wide, shading nurturing
us on our dusty way
We sit we dream we think, looking
back sixty and ten
Baby steps, lanky legs, long legged
colts, short pants
Timeworn apprentice learning the
arts, seafarer burnishing the trade
Father, grandpa passing it on, caring
son in those last declining days
Running east, running west,
running north running south
Ever running, returning full circle to
the start, emerging from where?
Returning to what? Looking forward
always, the next journey's step
Uplifting, nurturing, carrying,
helping, My Brother's Keeper

Dreams

Today I flew cross-country
Check the winds, hear the weather
Plot the route, watch the time
See the bridge, spy the train
Floating above, oops mind the bird
Today I thought of my father
Today I dreamt of my mother
Son, why do it?
I thought of Daniel Burnham
Civil Engineer Extraordinaire
I thought of Chicago, his dream
His plan, his work
His magic to stir men's blood
I dream, I fly
He dreams, he runs
She dreams, the preacher one
The nurse, the caring one, dreams on
Song bird, dancer, traveler,
New Yorker, dream on
Dolly, Ali, long gone, still alive
You brought us up, you let us go
No limits you set low
Thanks and Thanks to Parents Two
Merry Christmas and
Happy New Year to You

Hotel Heron

Today I arrived in Paradise
Not via the pearly gateway
But at the Heron entranceway
Long walk through the passageway
Paradise, no clouds, no angels winged
Aquarium blue, babbling, gurgling, willowing
Paneling dark, an era old Blighty evokes
Grecian column, Rubenesque, grotesque
Cherubim at desk, sweetly smiling
Greeting, writing, welcoming
Is this paradise, I'm thinking?
Nah, just an innkeeper's imaginings.

Marathon Man

Run, Run, Run, Ran, Ran, Ran
Marathon Man, Marathon Man
Run in school, that's cool
Run in Iere, so pretty
Run at sixty, in Miami
Vamos a Cuba, Vamos Habana
Visitar las primas, Encontrar la familia
Mi hermano deportiva
Un atleta maraton y historiador
Fly to Habana, Fly in Habana
White shoes, Nike sneaker
Hours two, fastest ever
Pheel, Pheel they shout, from
five k out
Mucha Comida, Muchas Bebidas
Con mucho gusto
Hola Cuba

A Winter's Morn

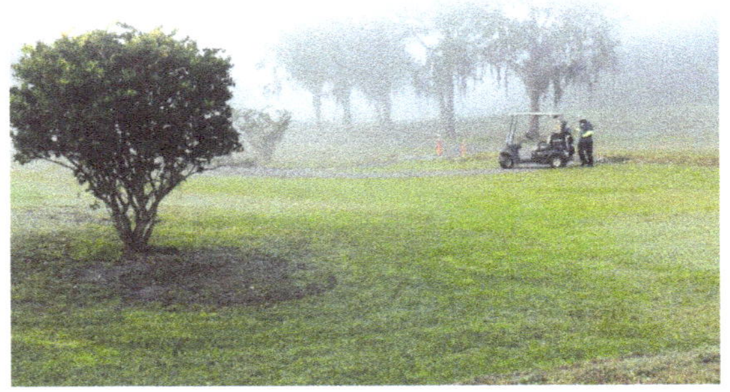

A winter's morning, golf course waiting
Frost lying, stretching o'er fairways, greens
Winter-like snow, lush green tees no
Stark trees stand out, no leaves just bare limbs
Far distant lonely evergreen, sentry-like stands alone

Soft sunlight bathes the forest, lighting, lightening
Faintly glowing, brushing over upright pines
One glorious shaft pierces east to west
A spotlight, a painting, bright spot at its best
Soft milky blue skies, now livening as Sol arises

No eclipse for me, he boasts: I rule the day, the most
Scotch bonnet, red pepper shiver, basil, tomato all quiver
Only Christmas cactus stands up proud, radiant
Red tipped flowers blooming, gloriously rising
Today a winter's morning in chapel wesley.

Goodbye

Crying, Crying, Screaming, Wailing
Today we are here, tomorrow where?
Grey skies gloaming, pink ribbon waving
Today we are here, tomorrow where?

Lifelong companion, fruit of womb
Today we are here, tomorrow where?
A husband, a son, gone to tomb
Today we are here, tomorrow where?

A song, a note, a plink, Tom Dooley
Today we are here, tomorrow where?
Hang down our heads, saddened truly
Today we are here, tomorrow where?

O Lord we cry, Why? Why?
Today we are here, tomorrow where?
What justice, what pain to die
Today we are here, tomorrow where?

Questions, questions, good people all
Today we are here, tomorrow where?
Should I bear this at all?
Today we are here, tomorrow where?

Sit and ponder, green leaves
Today we are here, tomorrow where?
Flowers sprouting, lush red berries
Today we are here, tomorrow where?

Whom did we touch along the way?
Today we are here, tomorrow where?
Leaving no mark, nay we say
Today we are here, tomorrow where?

Rising and leaving, upward bound
Today we are here, tomorrow where?
Climbing, climbing, angels bound
Today we are here, tomorrow where?

EARLY MORNING

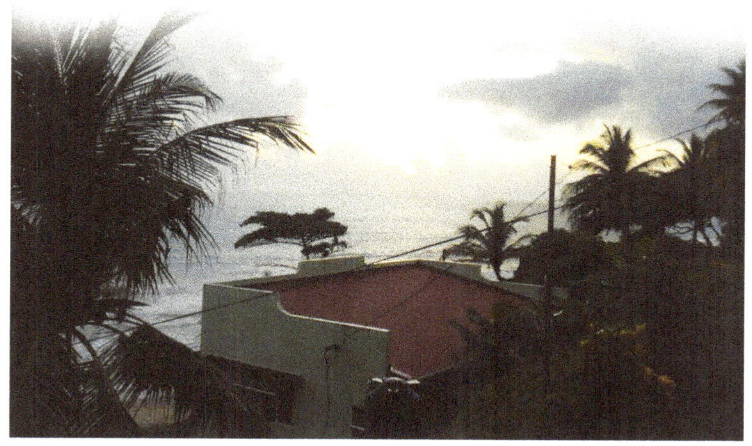

Sitting here on the front porch
Sipping a morning cup of tea
Gazing out at the green north hillside
Rising sun coming over the hill
Warm, bright sunshine streaming over the rooftops
Birds, pair by pair swiftly flying
Perching, tweeting, chirping
Yellow colors flashing past against the green
Good Morning Cascade, all is well

Give Thanks

Thanksgiving, national, international
Preparation before, by all for all
Visitors by car, Georgia state neighbor so far
Riverview south, county Hillsboro so near
Septuagenarians, teenagers, friends all here
Soccer playing, swimming, mama drives them all
Menu on the mind, turkey, sweetbread, ham
Stuffing, gravy, rolls, veggies, crockpot, salmon
But wait, we need to add beef and stew, soufflé
Sweet potato, salad, beet and red, plantanos
Gungo peas and rice. Mac and cheese, gosh
We ain't touch dessert yet, drinks first
Sorrel, hibiscus flowers, ginger beer and pineapple
Apple juice, natural, wine, rosé, white petillant
Brandy, milk, ice crushed and cubes, tinkling
Football, soccer, tv wide, ole time kaiso jamming, jamming
Rest for now, sated first round, table still laden
Contemplating apple pie,
Christmas pudding
Yes, is still Thanksgiving, but is Trini, Jamaica
Sierra Leone, for rum ball we waiting, we waiting

Give thanks for friends, give thanks for family
Give thanks for life, give thanks for land
Give thanks for earth, give thanks for birth
Give thanks, give thanks, Give thanks O Lord, O Lord.

Wondrous

How wondrous are you O God
Full red sorrel petals, sole slender branch
Pink flowers open to the soft grey sky
Drop of water resting at tip of leaf

Palm trees drooping, waving gentle
In unseen breeze. Lo sunlight streaks and breaks
Glowing brief on lake and lawn,
Incessant drip of water as we sit, sipping morning cup

Christmas cactus blooms pink and rose
Green shoots adorning potted plants
Old wind-stirred leaves flutter and drop
Twin birds flash by, harmony of light

Grey-domed vault in heaven high above
Trees yet stirring, responding, branches twisting
Hawk landing, plucking, balancing feeding
Thank God for light and love and life.

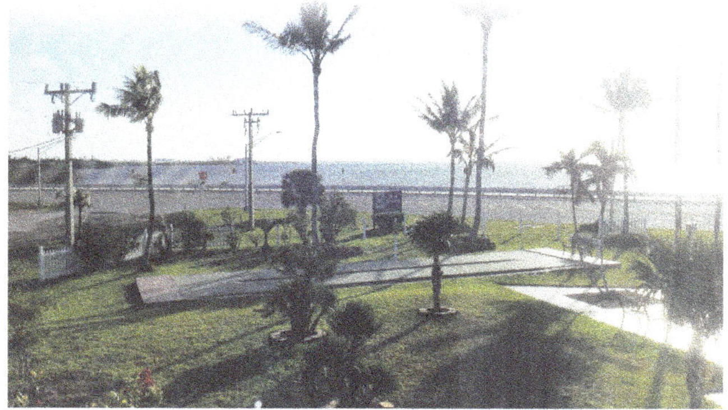

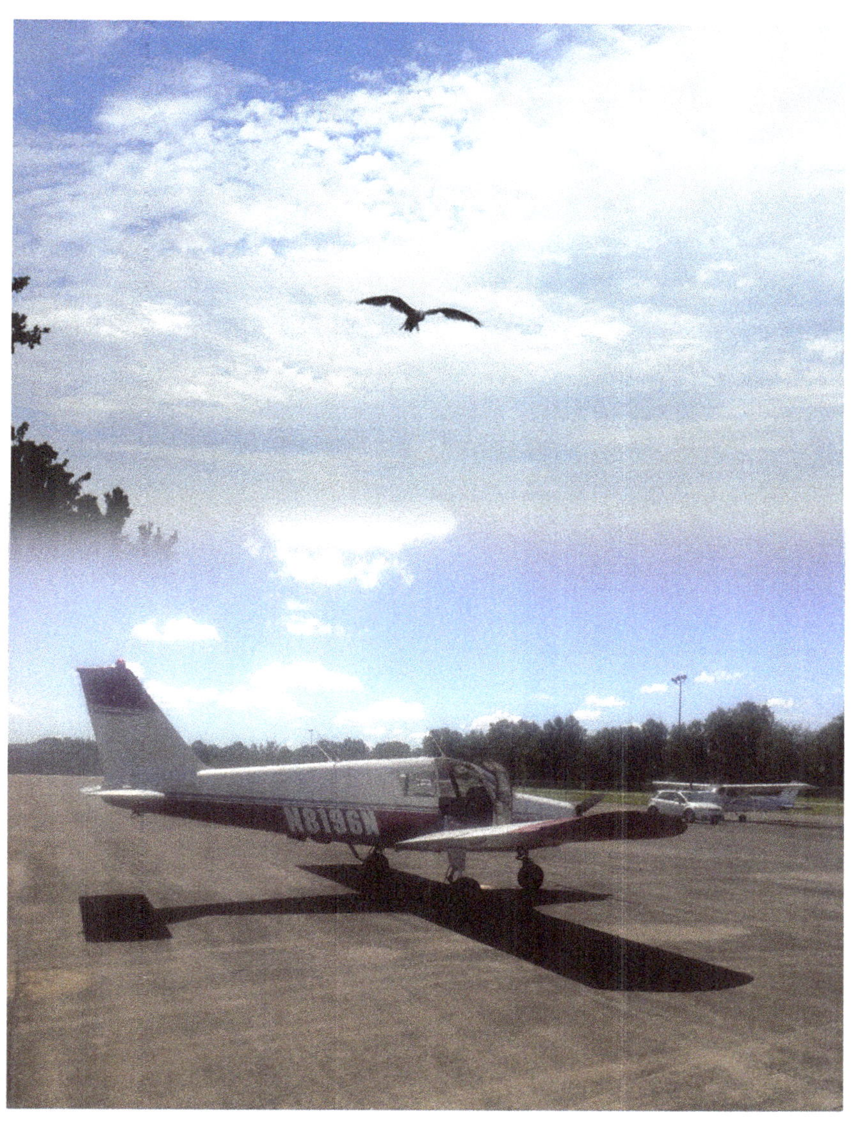

– Growth –

Solo

Today yuh boy solo
Dolly, Ali, yuh boy solo
He gorn up in plane by he self
And he come down, by he self
Yuh boy solo

Wake up today easy easy
Going to fly, no big ting
Just cruising, not thinking
Another day, fly with instructor
Up down, up down, round and round

Zephyrhills Airport, hello Bill, hello Katie
Today yuh solo, if yuh want
Huh? Ah ready? What if?
Ok, together we go
Up down, up down, round and round
We fly, we stall
Not nice that one, but we stall again
Come in to land and go around
We touch down, Bill hops out
Yuh on yuh own baby

Gliders to the right, jumpers to the left
Deltas below, Cessna behind
Yuh on yuh own baby
Take off, climb, turn, land
Take off, climb, turn, land
I did it, I did it
Today yuh boy solo

Flying 101

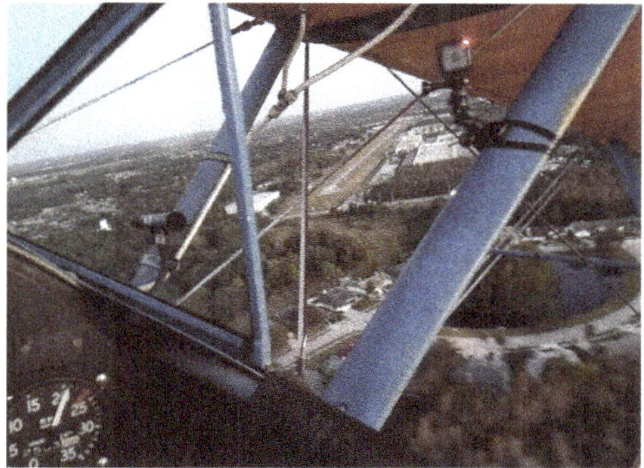

Photo courtesy of Catherine Frey

Soaring on high thru cloud and sky
From Zephyrhills to Crystal River on high
Cold front approaching, winds gusting
Short field on turf, takeoff and landing

Divert she says, Dunellon afar
Steep turns, slow flight, good so far
Blinders on, emergency landing
Go around, still twisting and tossing

VOR to track, find our way home
Turning and turning round a dome
There's the field, crosswinds abound
Runway 18 power on, so safe the ground

The paperwork abounds, fill in the dots
Show the passport, verify the lot
At last the privileged certificate
Congrats, you're a pilot, my mate

Pendant

Depending before me in all its glory
Aubergine so noble, so full, so lovely
Huggable, eatable, desi-rable
I look, I drool, lips water, so cookable

Today I admire my handiwork
Tilled with fork like country folk
Sprayed with misty Cascade rain
This fruit grew with no pain

A thing of beauty, so long, so full
Hanging, inviting, we long to pull
Rejoicing, approaching, lips smacking
Wip, wap, we send it packing

Low simmering pot on coals so hot
Yonder purple skin, compost your lot
Inner beauty, a meal is seen
A tribute to noble aubergine

BIRDS

Today I heard a hawk
An early morning squawk
Twice repeated, waking me
Arise, come see, aloft on peak

Through the door, news to seek
With camera in hand, I did leap
A bird, a hawk roof atop
Interloper the sparrow thought
Whirl and dive, 'tis my spot

Serene he sat, quiet at rest
Flew then to woods not west
No fuss, unhurried, wings that beat
To greet the majesty of the east.

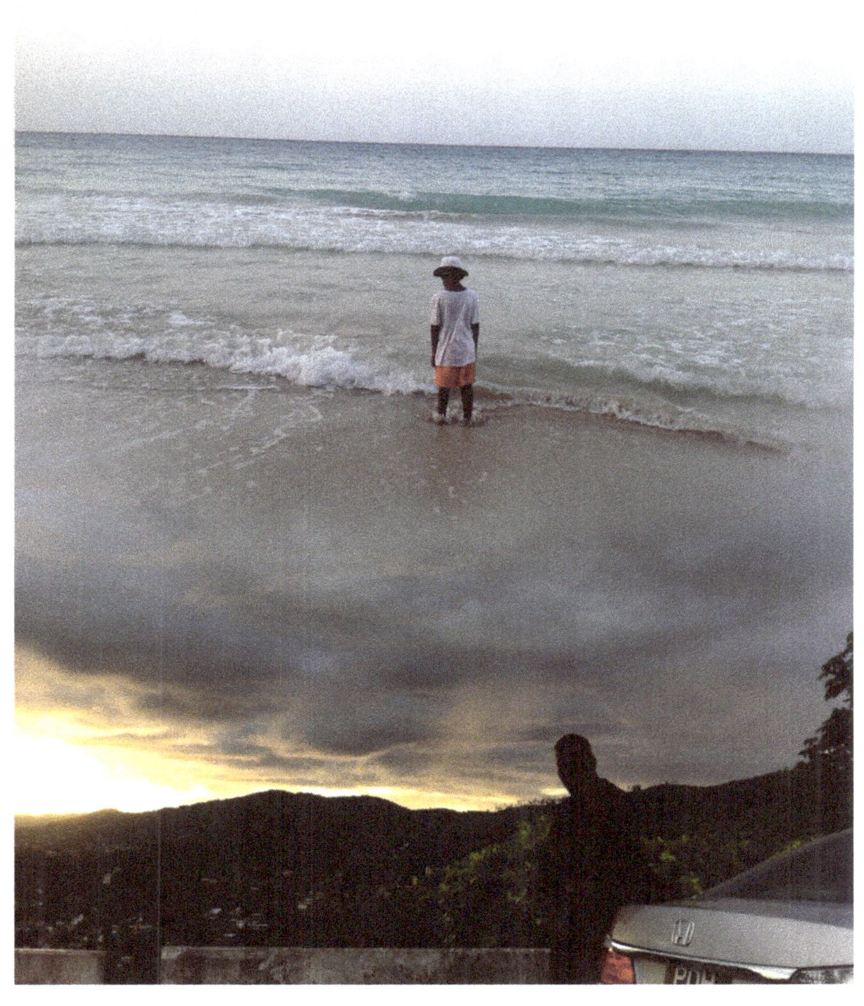

— EXPERIENCE —

Over the Years

Over the years I've seen many sights
Over the years I've loved many loves
Over the years I've led many lives
Over the years I've told many truths
Over the years I've told many lies
Over the years I've been faithless
Over the years I've been thoughtless

Looking back there are many regrets
But, truth be told I'd not change any of it
Circumstances dictated words and actions
Pulling together many strands, untangling,
Reweaving into new patterns, new outlooks
New unknown directions leading to today

To those I've hurt and they are many
Scars remain forever etched in my heart
To those who garnered joy and love
Thanks for letting me be part of you
To those I have not known, an infinite number
There is still time for us to get together
To those who read this, they may be few
Thanks for Love, to your own self be true

THE PATH NOT TAKEN

We heard of each other before meeting; not old friends
But parents who had their own relationships, hidden secrets
T'was a summer dance, music blasting, my very own anthem
The joyous, joyful theme song, Lloyd Price Mister Personality

We met, walked and smiled in the Rock Gardens
Carifesta it was, the very first one, like young love
Music, poetry, dance filled the air, yellow poui abloom
Tall, elegant, shy, bold, beautiful, flaring flowery skirt

The Park, a circle broad and tree'd, elegant stately houses
Set back, carriage house detached, shingled dovecot atop
Many a long trek to visit, past the bridge, Norris at home watching
Welcomed by Mom, oh how did young love, innocent blossom

First drive, new license proudly showing off in Dad's car
Western Main Road, Point Cumana, Amow's Hill our stop
The sea view, brown water at the house gently lapping
Childhood memories of vacations, family, the boys liming

Ah young blissful love. Oh oh, mechanical troubles abound
What to do, can't call Dad, he'd laugh and say you fix it
Head in bonnet bravely, poking, pushing, not knowing
Hi Dad, just channeled you, click, smiling it's good to go.

Then like Eden, the old wily serpent appears and whispers
The Tree of Knowledge lies in the center, the Mother Country
To old, cold England send the sweet young luscious flower
To finish, make perfect the perfect, upward mobility they say

Heartbroken we part, drifting ships that briefly touched
Will we meet again, how, when and where, wherever, ever?
Will fragile love rekindle, will we fight, feel betrayed?
The past the influencer of the present, the future forever

We change, we meet again, forgiven and forgiving
Touch and bloom, procreate lovingly, roundly like Beyoncé
And yet parents who had their own relationships, hidden secrets
Lead to pain filled choices, immeasurable future, present joys.

The Bubble

'Boon they say, grimace as they spy you
Rounding the corner, no greeting, no 'mornin
A bubble holding tight preconceptions
Worthless blackness the only thought evermore

Shouting in the void of mindlessness, captured
By that thin membrane, that skin that informs
All feeling, that container holding together tightly
No osmosis, let nothing in, keeping Them out
Rising with the air, blown by the wind, wherever
Resting lightly, not letting go, admiring grudgingly
Feats of sporting brawn, used and abused, enslaved
As in days of yore, striving to keep good men out
We do not know you, wish not to see you, not
One of us, no culture, no mores, animals alone
Keep out of my bubble, poof, burst, disappear
You know what, We here, not going anywhere.

Welcome Home

Standing in de line, warm welcome sun
Diverse faces, Chinese, Indian, Old, Gray
Tired, weary, waiting patiently, quietly
Toddler running, screaming, pushcart playing
Distraught group to one side; Voice suddenly booming
Dey need an address; Laventille he says
Dey need an address; Up de Hill he says
Dey need an address; Voice patiently explaining
Street, house number; Oh she says doubtfully
Use my grandmother's old house
But nobody living dey now,
Never mind, write it down
Yuh come from foreign
Welcome home, Fellow Trini

Requiem In Pace

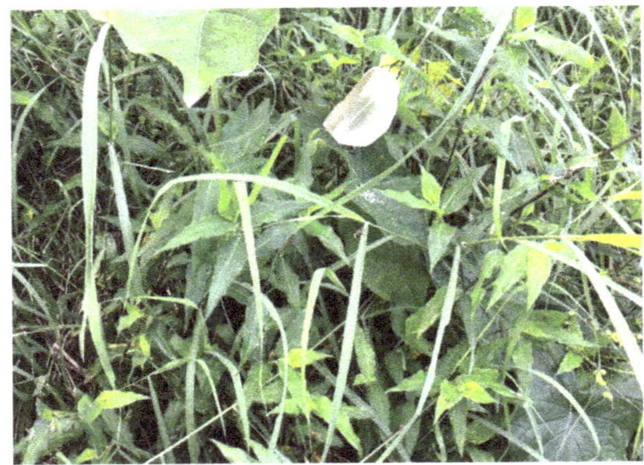

The evening shadows lengthen as we sit and watch
The neighbors depart for the far far north
No shouts of fore, no golfers in colorful plumage
And even more colorful language in the looming dust

A slow death, progress for all, protests by all
But hearings, debates, rezoning, repaving for all
Deplorable my dears, we sit and wait
Missing the short skirts, finding the lost balls

Greenkeepers now tend the weeds
Drilling like midwives for new birth, scraping cancerous chemo
Removing interred pesticide, preparing for new life –
Houses, rising like tombstones, in cimiterie Lapeyrouse

Today the distant woodpecker, sound throbbing, nock nock
Silent hawk perched upright, motionless on the high peak
Small shadows from solitary trees, isolated clusters bathed
In the rising sun, still flourishing, living breathing but waiting

A giant of a man we knew, small in stature, big in heart
An expanse of earth we knew, spreading before us
Wide and green. a man's lifetime with so much pleasure
So much good work—dead to rise again

Love

Love is holding hands
When he no longer recognizes you
Love is giving your kids
Piggyback rides visiting in prison
Love is hugging your dad
When you see him, smiling, caring
Love is fond memories
When long lost friends meet anew
Love is a gentle touch
Love is

— **LAGNIAPPE** —
(Freebie)
Poetry Through the Lens

SIGHTS OF
TRINIDAD AND TOBAGO

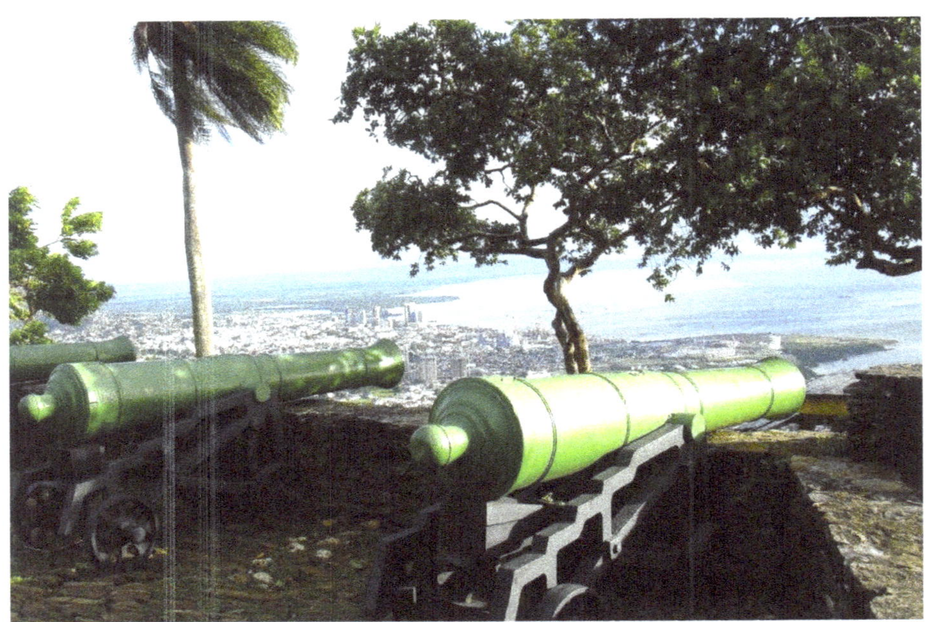

The Cannon – Fort George overlooking Port of Spain

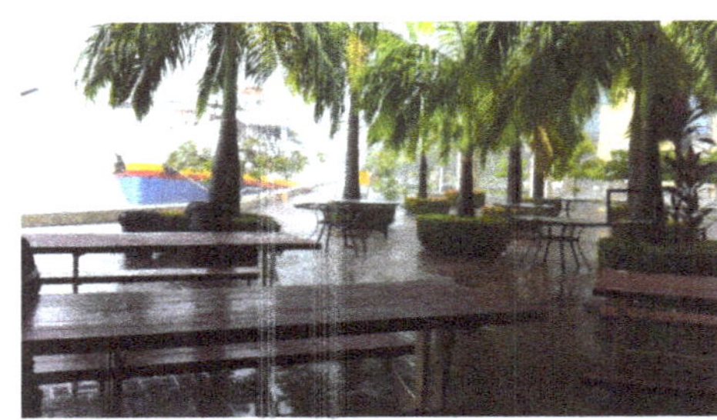

Rainy Day at the Breakfast Shed,
Port of Spain Waterfront

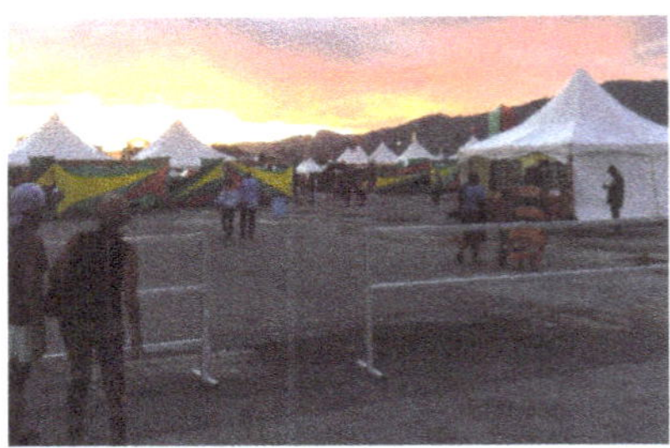

Sunset at Emancipation Village,
Queens Park Savannah

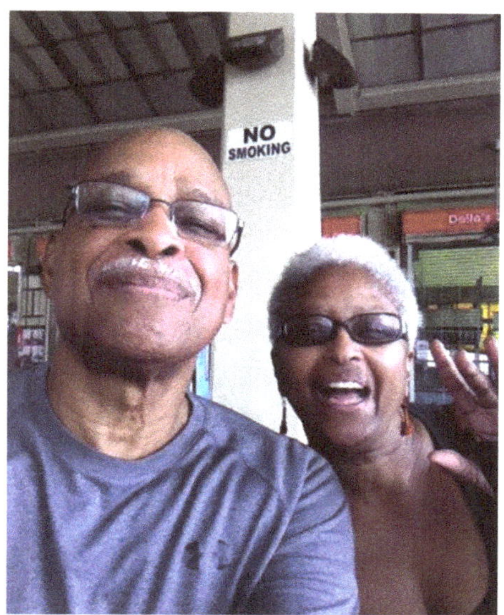

Belly Full – Bake and Shark,
Breakfast Shed

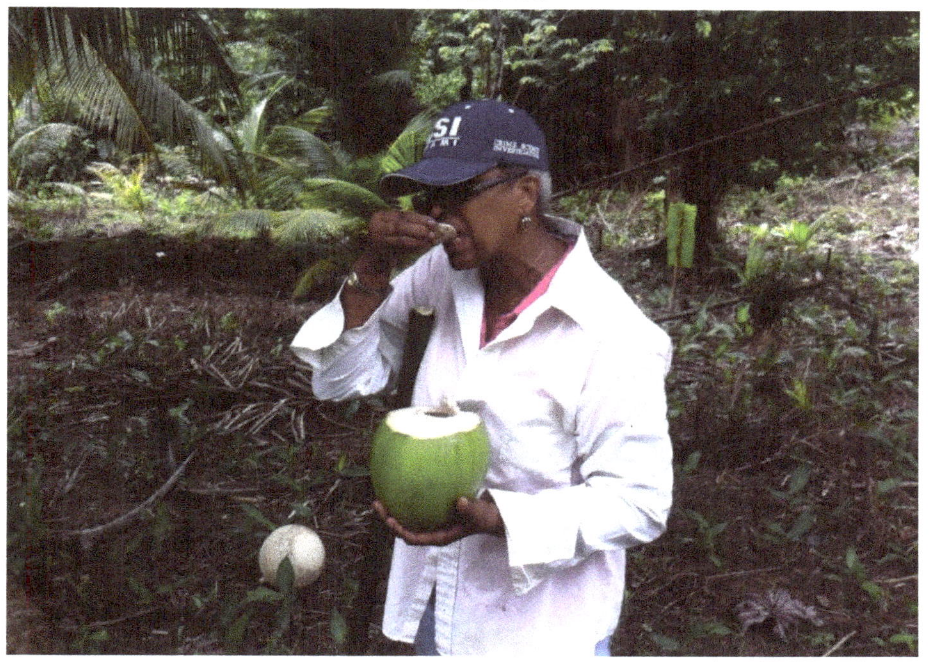

Organic Coconut Water, Toco

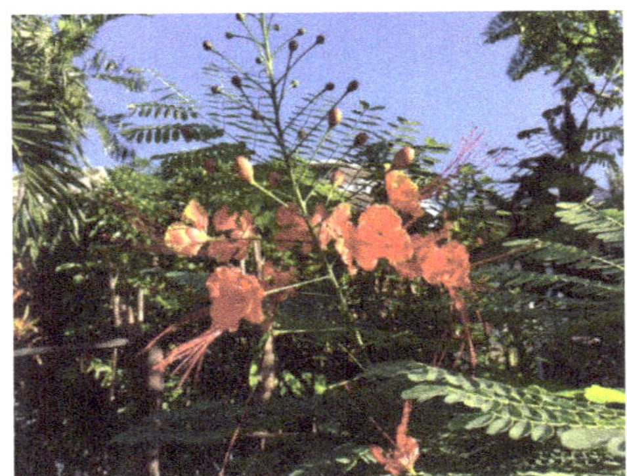

Flamboyant - Early Morning Walk,
Cascade

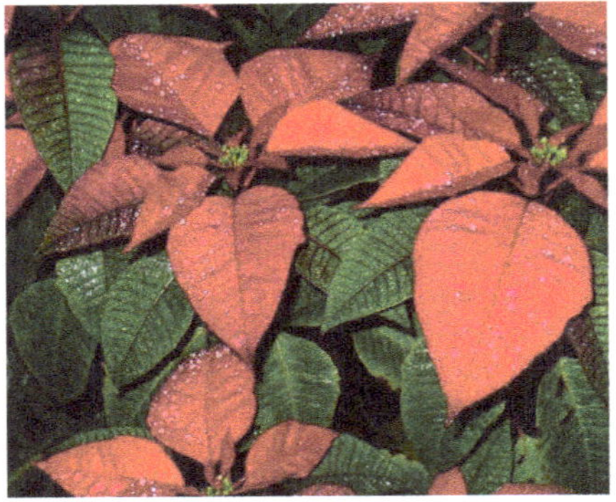

Dew on Christmas Poinsettia

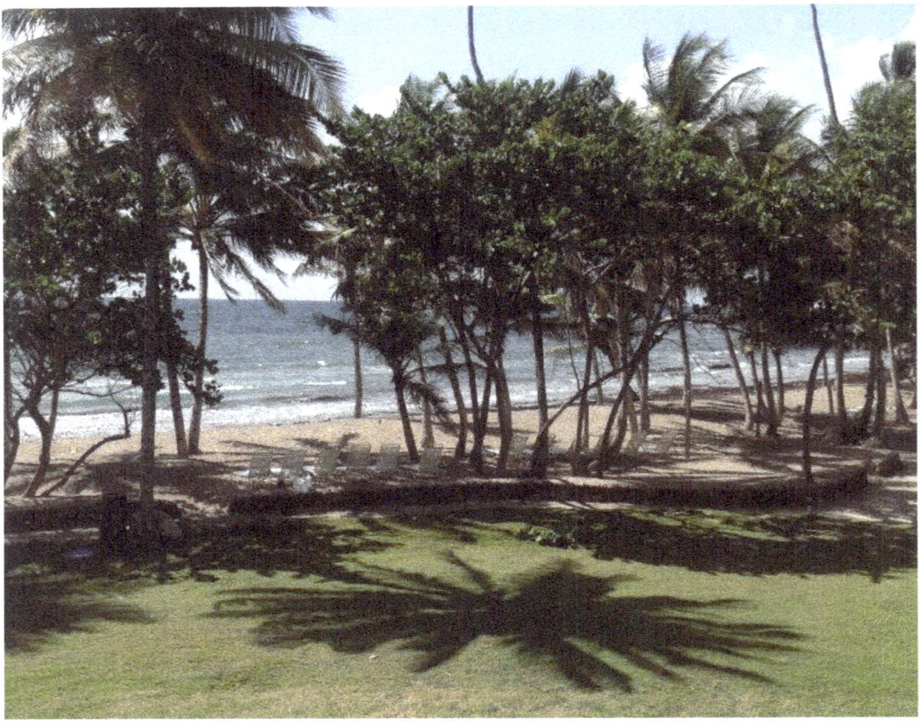

Sunrise – Magdalena, Tobago

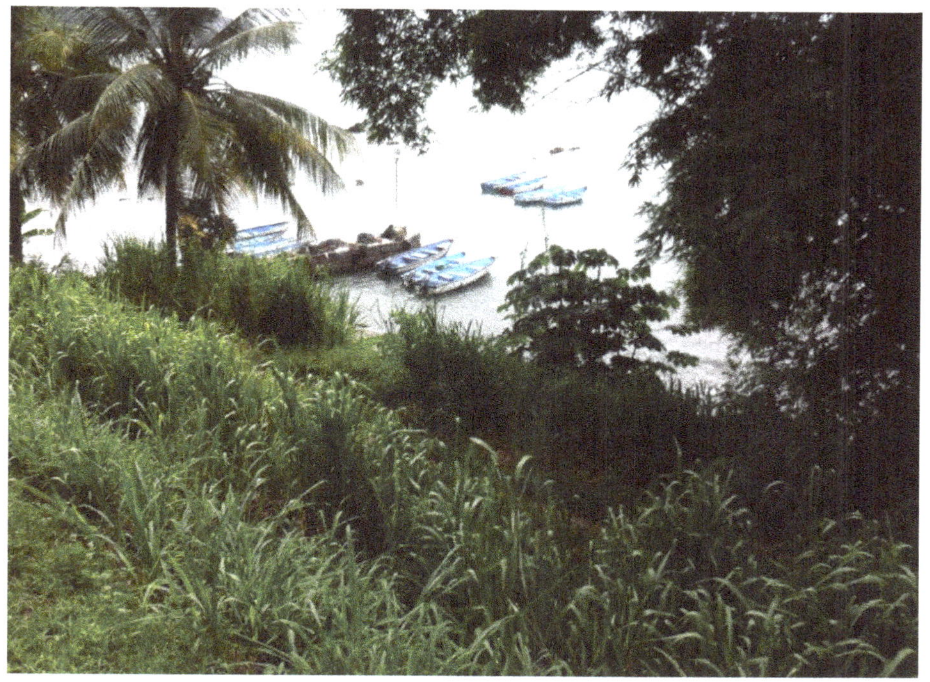

Fisherman's Rest, Toco

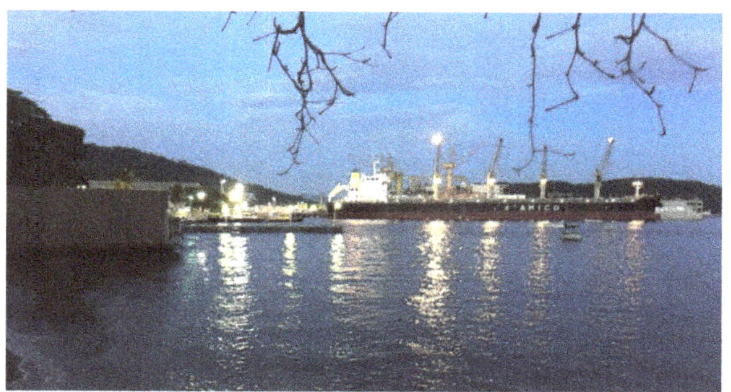

Dusk – Chaguaramus, Gulf of Paria

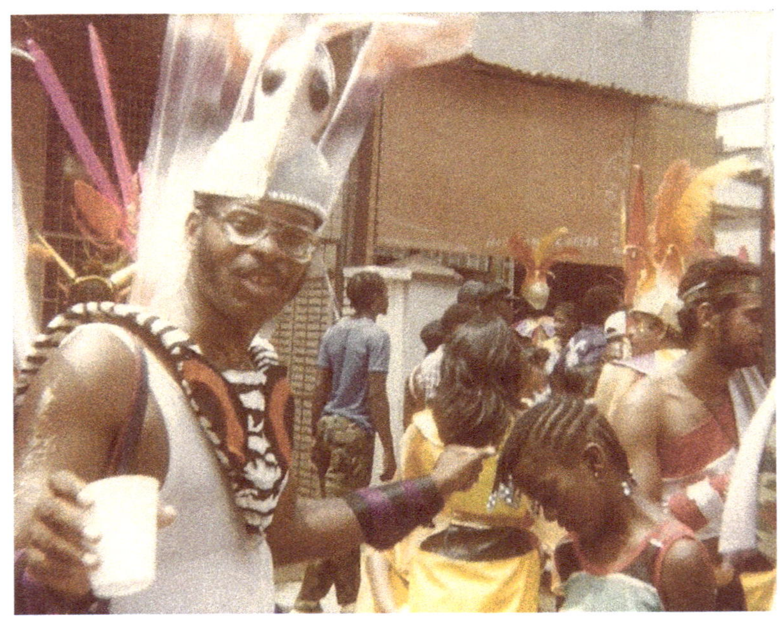

Trinidad Carnival – Having a Good, Good Time

TRAVELS

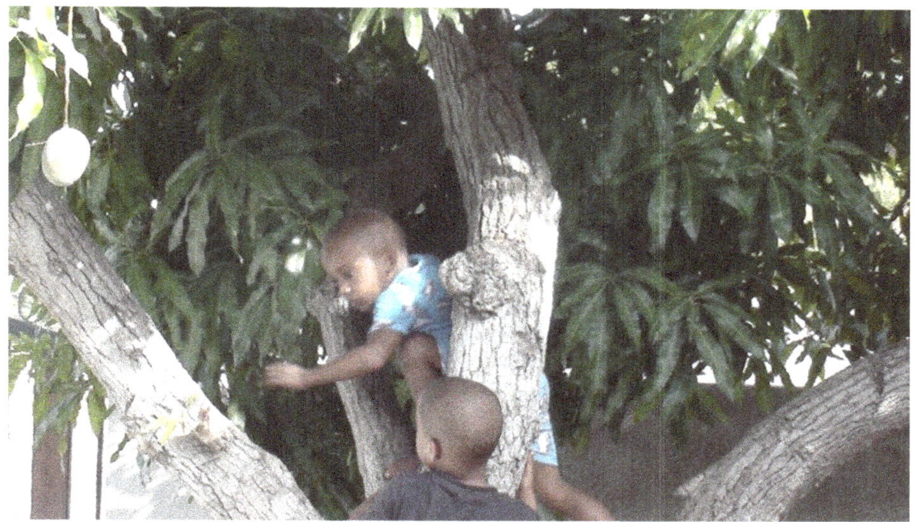

Climbing the Mango Tree – Spanish Town, Jamaica

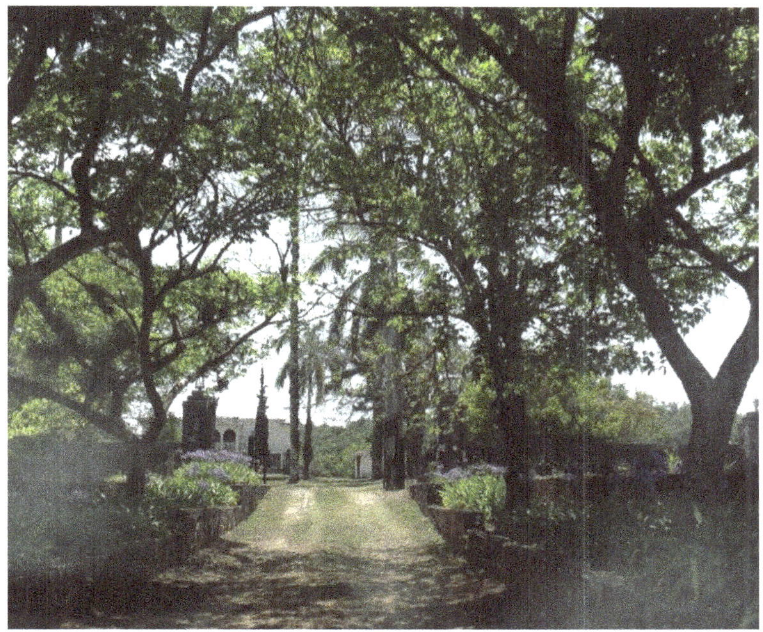

Welcome to Lillyfield, Jamaica

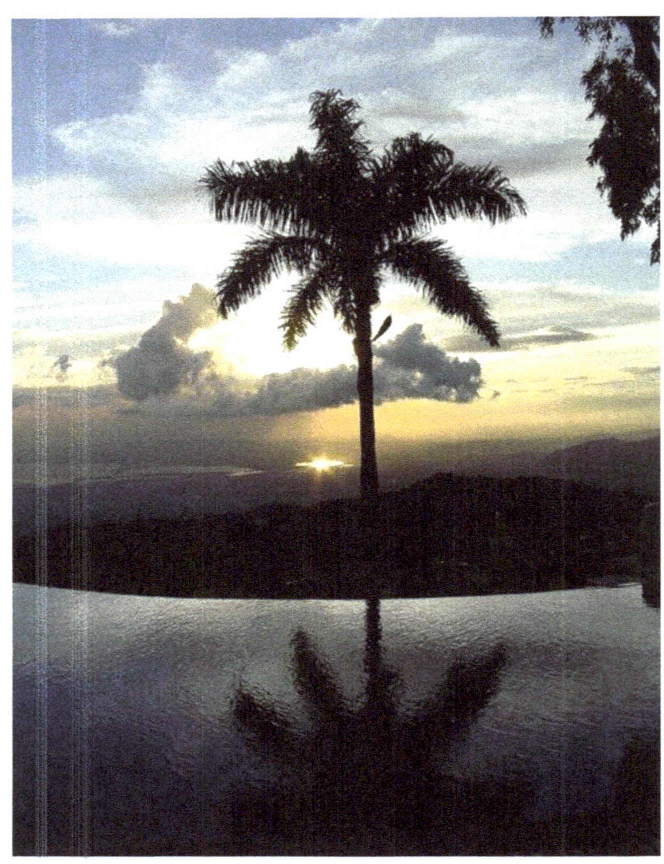

Sunset over Kingston – Strawberry Hill, Jamaica

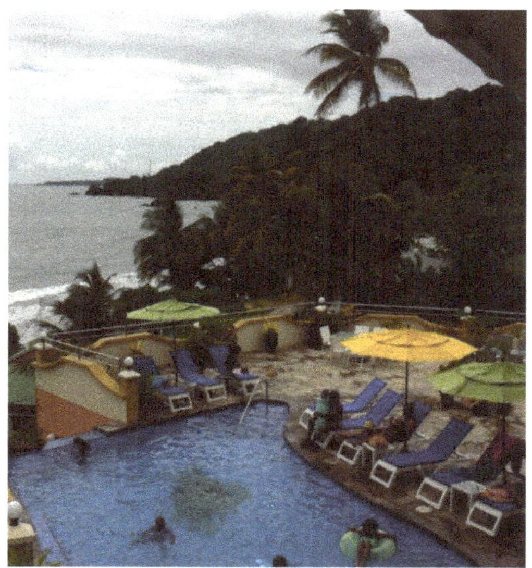

Anise Resort – San Souci, Trinidad

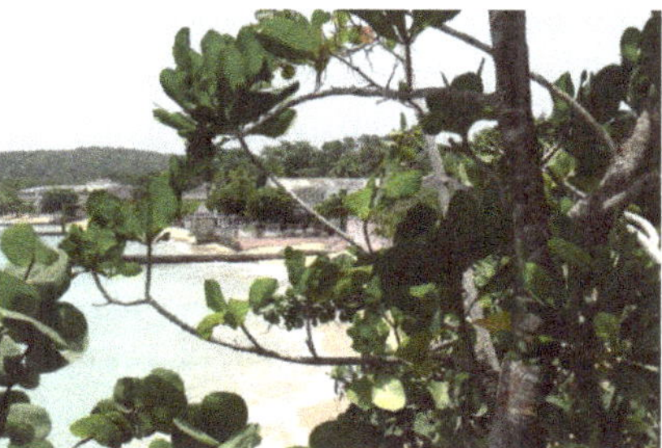

The Restless Sea – Golden Sands, Jamaica

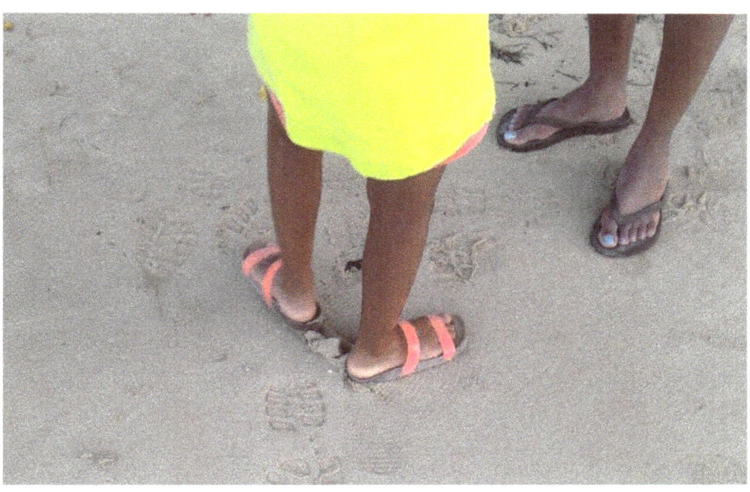

Beach Wear, Ocho Rios Style, Jamaica

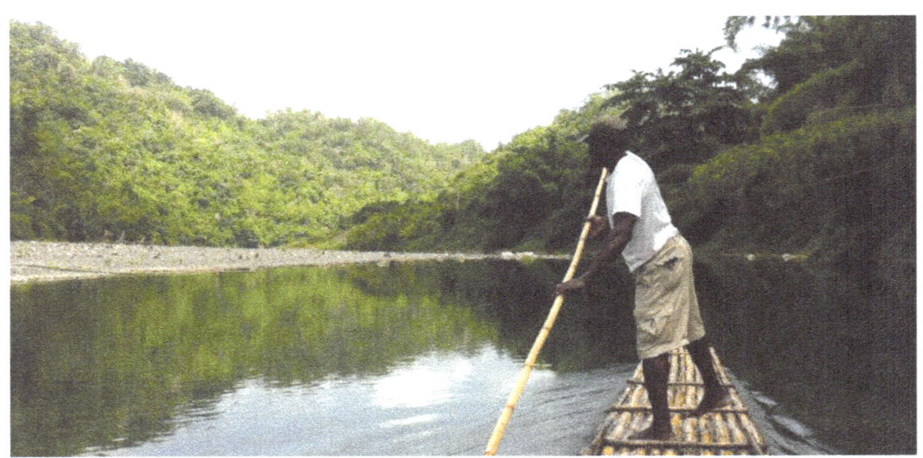

Rafting down the Rio Grande, Jamaica

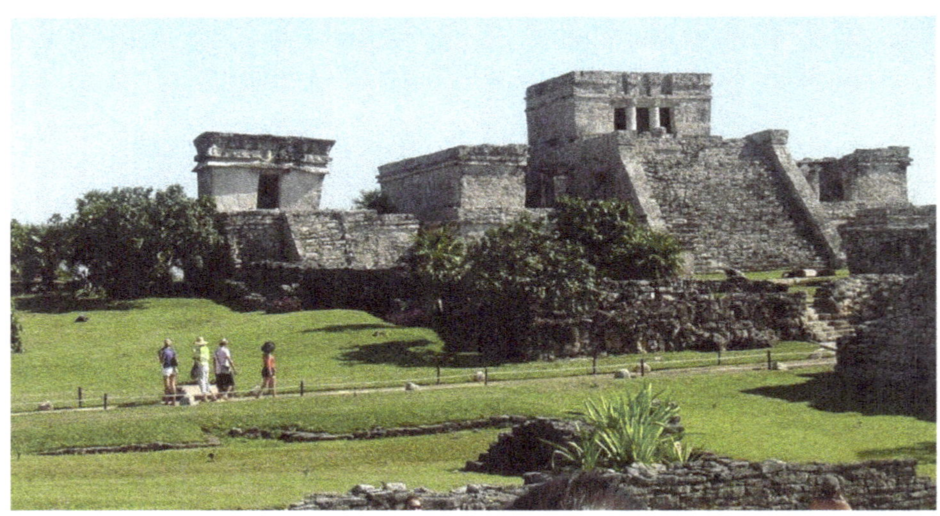

El Castille – Tulum, Mexico

HOME IN FLORIDA

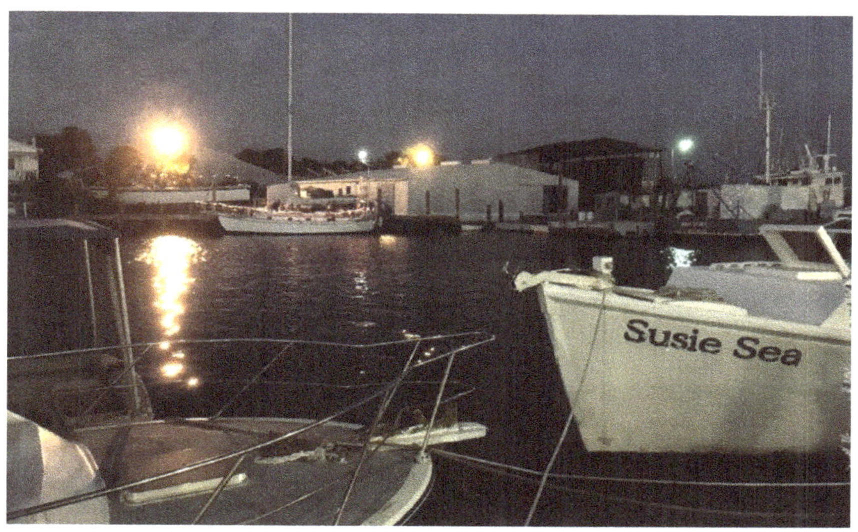

Evening walk on the Bayou, Florida

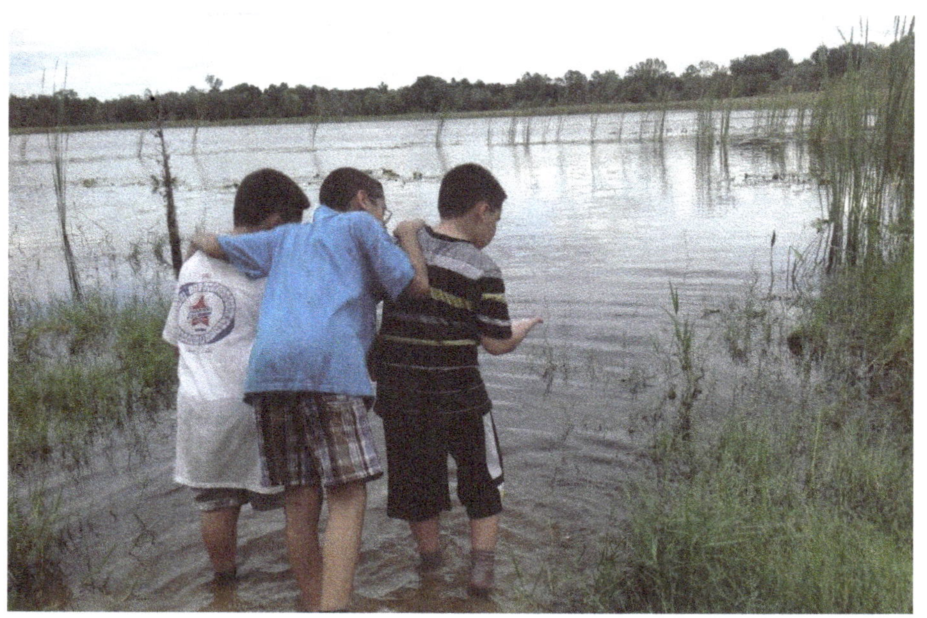

What is it? Lake Park, Florida

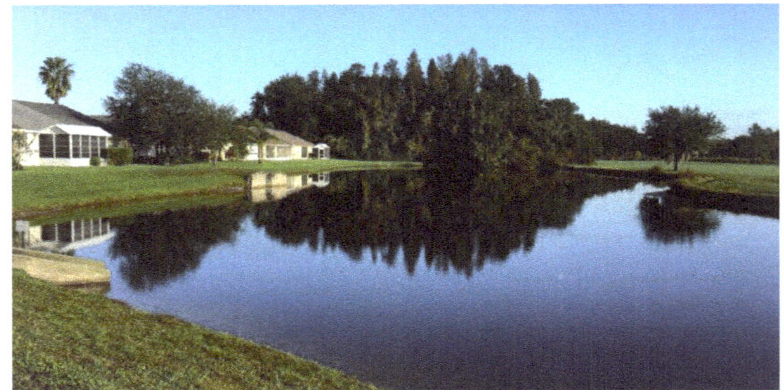

Reflections - Gentle Ben, Florida

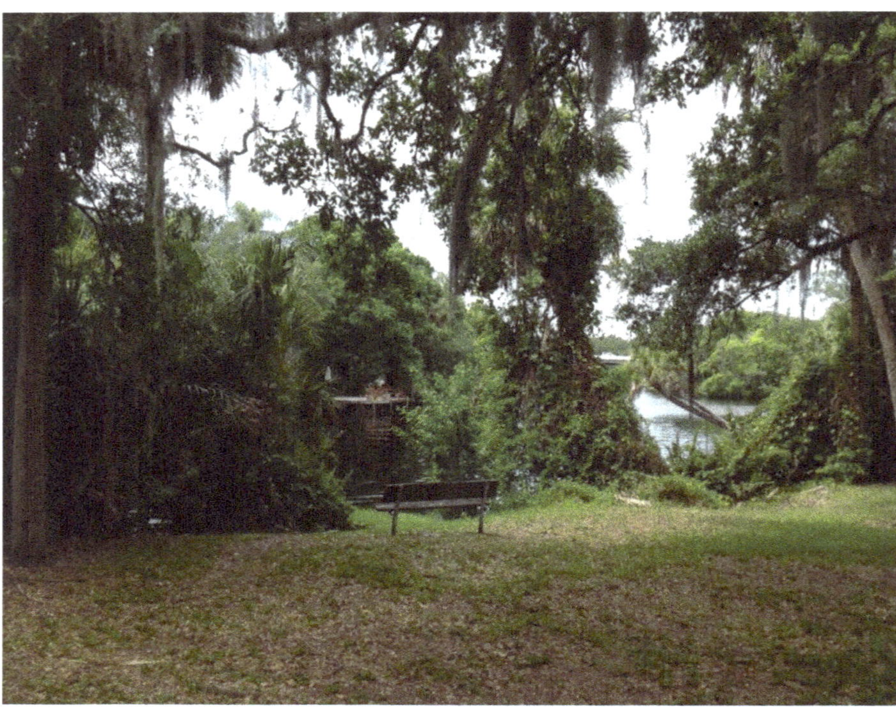

Hillsborough River – River Tower Park, Florida

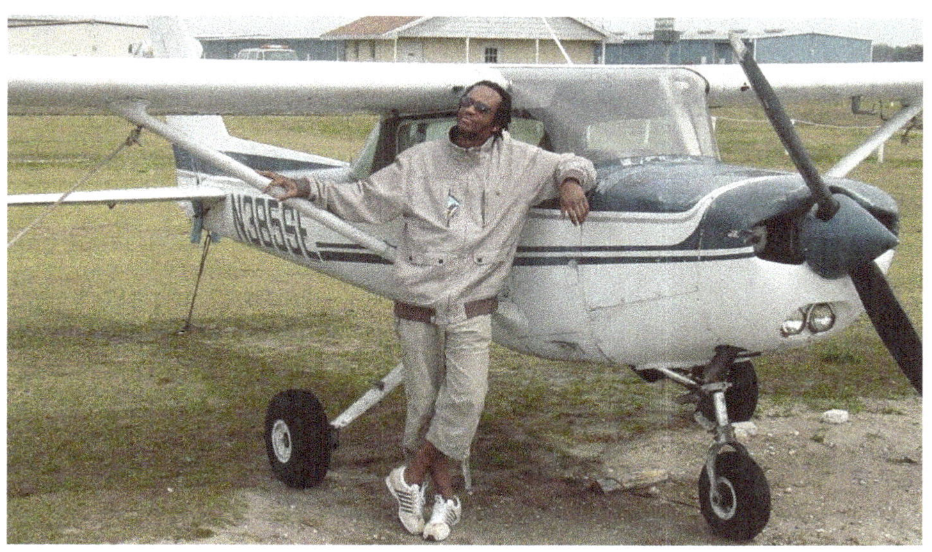

Dreams of Flying, Florida